THE CHANGING FACES OF

Cowley

BOOK THREE

Carole Newbigging
Susanne Shatford
Trevor Williams

Robert Boyd
PUBLICATIONS

Published by
Robert Boyd Publications
260 Colwell Drive
Witney, Oxfordshire OX8 7LW

First published 1999

Copyright © Carole Newbigging,
Susanne Shatford, Trevor Williams and
Robert Boyd Publications

ISBN: 1 899536 47 7

TITLES IN THE *CHANGING FACES* SERIES

Banbury: Book One
The Bartons
Bicester: Book One *and* Book Two
Bladon with Church Hanborough and
   Long Hanborough
Botley and North Hinksey: Book One
   and Book Two
Chipping Norton: Book One
St Clements and East Oxford:
   Book One *and* Book Two
Cowley: Book One, Book Two *and*
   Book Three
Cowley Works: Book One
Cumnor and Farmoor with Appleton
   and Eaton
St Ebbes and St Thomas: Book One
   and Book Two
Eynsham: Book One *and* Book Two
Faringdon and surrounding villages
Grimsbury
Headington: Book One *and* Book Two
Iffley
Jericho: Book One *and* Book Two
Kennington
Littlemore and Sandford

Marston: Book One *and* Book Two
North Oxford: Book One *and* Book Two
Oxford City Centre: Book One
South Oxford: Book One *and* Book Two
Summertown and Cutteslowe
West Oxford
Witney: Book One
Wolvercote with Wytham and Godstow
Woodstock: Book One *and* Book Two
Yarnton with Cassington and Begbroke

FORTHCOMING

Abingdon
Banbury: Book Two
Blackbird Leys
Charlbury
Cowley Works: Book Two
Easington
Florence Park
Grimsbury: Book Two
Littlemore and Sandford: Book Two
Oxford City Centre: Book Two
Rose Hill
Thame
Witney: Book Two

Printed and bound in Great Britain at The Alden Press, Oxford

Contents

Front cover photograph
VJ Fancy Dress Party in Wilkins Road.

Back cover photograph
A pram race believed to be August Bank Holiday 1983. This group, organised by John McKiernan, set off from the Nuffield Arms in Littlemore Road, Cowley, for a race round six public houses, ending up at the Jolly Postboys in Florence Park. The winning team was the Colonel Hall Chasers.

Acknowledgements

The authors are most grateful to the organisations and individuals through whose kindness the photographs in this book were made available. In particular we wish to thank:

Maurice Allen	Wendy Angell
Pam Ball	Mick Ball
Margaret Bargus	Mrs Blizzard and John Bennett
Mike Brogden	Haydn Cooper
Edna Cornell	Alan Cross
Palmetto Cullimore	Malcolm Davies
Una Dean	Haydn Evans
Deirdre Foster	Clifford Gooch
Eileen Hayes	Rosemary Ledger
Rick Lee	Rosemary Marshall
Bob Newton	Linda Peach
June Poole	Philip Powley
Ruth Racey	E and M Radburn
Peris Roberts	Dorothy Slack
John Stead	Thelma Telling
Joyce Titchell	Ray Titchell
Don White	Nancy White
John White	Bob Whitford
John Vivien	

Christopher Hobbs for information on John Bunyan Church;
Margaret Batey and Sister Anne Darwin for information about Our Lady's R.C. School;
Netta Simpkins and Carol Cherry for Church Cowley St James School;
Kathy Turner for St Christopher's School;
Helen Thomas and Rosanne Butler for Donnington School;
Wendy White of Templars Square Management;
Keith Price, Newsquest (Oxford) Limited;
Nuala La Vertue, Oxfordshire Photographic Archive at the Centre for Oxfordshire Studies;
Reed Information Service for permission to extract from Kelly's Directories.

Particular thanks to Sheila Tree for generously providing material for the section on the Florence Park Estate, from part of a much larger collection. It is planned to publish a separate book - *The Changing Faces of Florence Park* - in the foreseeable future. Anyone with further material relating to this area is invited to contact Sheila Tree c/o Robert Boyd Publications.

Clubs and Recreation

Demolition of Bedford House August 1960.

This was the original home of the Cowley Community Association which was formed in 1949. A new Community Centre was built across the road, at a cost of £75,000, and this became home to the Community Association in 1964. The first phase of the new Community Centre was completed in April 1962, consisting of a workshop and cloakroom on the ground floor and a multi-purpose hall on the first floor. The second phase consisted of a main hall, the Community Association accommodation and the youth club. These two buildings were linked by a bridge. The stage within the main hall was fully equipped for dramatics and two staircases lead down to the dressing rooms. In 1965 membership of the Community Association was 600 adults and over 70 young people and subscriptions were 2s 6d a year. The new Community Centre provided facilities for various groups, including drama, choir, orchestra, dressmaking, art, car maintenance, woodwork and the Workers Educational Association. There were also clubs for chess, cine, old people, old-time and ballroom dancing and travel abroad.

Cowley Community Association

Youth Club

Although the Association had reservations with regard to starting a youth club, it was formed in 1957 under the leadership of Dot and Tom Wellstood, who had previously been involved in Bullingdon Youth Club, Peat Moors. The Club ran on Friday evenings in a room behind Bedford House, the Association Headquarters.

Tom and Dot Wellstood took a back seat in 1958 and became assistants to Norman Finnerty and Tom became manager of the football team. The formation of an Under 16 team in 1959 laid the foundations for a strong youth football squad. Tom and Dot Wellstood took over the running of the Club again from Norman Finnerty in 1960 and it moved into the new Community Centre buildings across the road.

The Youth Club's main outdoor activities were football and cricket. In the 1961–62 season the Under 18 football team won the Oxon. Youth League, Youth Cup and the Bicester Minor Cup, while the cricket team reached the final of the Boys' Clubs six-a-side competition in 1961 and 1962, taking the title in 1961.

Tom Wellstood's dedication to the football team was equalled by Dot's enthusiasm as number one supporter, washer of the kit and generally 'mother' to the boys. Tom and Dot handed over the running of the Club to Colin Greenop, the Club's first full-time leader, in 1963.

The Under 16 team, 1959–60 season. Left to right, back row: Ivor Holloway, Terry Wellstood, Bob Light, Martin Mascock, Alan Davis, Graham McKenzie, Tom Wellstood. Front row: Mick Webb, Terry Twine, Dave Barrett, Eddie Brewster, Bob Frankham.

The successful Under 18 Team 1961-62 season, winners of the Oxfordshire Youth League Youth Cup and Bicester Minor Cup. Left to right back row: Ron Strange (assistant manager), Nigel Calvert, Mick Webb, John Bowerman, Roy Pyniger, Barry Strange, Terry Wellstood, Tom Wellstood (manager). Front row: Nigel Strange (mascot), Alan Lacey, Alan Davis, Trevor Williams, Alan Bunting, Terry Twine. Inset: Dot Wellstood.

To honour the football teams' success in the 1961-62 season the Community Centre held a celebration supper for players and friends. Players at the back: John Bowerman, Roy Pyniger. Front row: Dickie Wotton, Alan Davis, Trevor Williams, Pete Jacobson, Terry Wellstood, Nigel Calvert, Barry Strange.

The Drama Group

The drama group flourished in the original Bedford House premises. At that time Peter Welch was warden of the Centre and was an active participant. This photograph of 1958 shows a proud moment for the Drama Group when the playwright, William Douglas Home, attended their performance of his *Reluctant Debutante*.

The Reluctant Debutante
CAST

Jimmy Broadbent	Ken Page
Sheila Broadbent (His Wife)	Beryl Wiggins
Jane (His Daughter)	J. Mary Hodnett
Mabel Crosswaite	Elizabeth Blake
Clarissa (Her Daughter)	Ann Kirby
David Bullock	Roy Hanlon
David Hoylake-Johnson	Bill Dabs
Mrs. Edgar	Marjorie Pipkin

The cast list for *The Reluctant Debutante*, performed on Saturday 1 November 1958 in the Cowley Community Centre Hall, Hockmore Street. Admission was 2s 6d.

Old Time Dancing in the old Bedford House hall c1958. Couples from the back to the front: Mrs Cook, –; Mrs Morgan, Dave Morgan; –, –; –, Arthur Griffiths; –, Les Brogden; –, –; Hilda Griffiths extreme left. These premises were the original home of the Youth Club.

Cowley Workers

Demolition of the original Village House, home to the Cowley Workers' Club, on the corner of Oxford Road and Between Towns Road, March 1971.

The Cowley Workers, it is said, was formed by six people who left the Cowley Conservative Club to form a new club for working men. The Club opened on 31 May 1929. The Club's first president was Harold Turner, a local carrier. He was one of a band of seven who met in the Village House on 15 April 1929, when the decision to set up the club was taken. Others at this meeting were Joe Pocock, Harry Pruce, Trevor Jones, Bill Wilkinson, H R Smith and Claude Roche. Bill Laitt and Cliff Martin were founder members at a time when subs were two shillings a year and beer was about sixpence a pint.

Other well-remembered officers of the Club were Alf Walker, Dick Abbott and Dave Murphy, all three trustees of the Club when it celebrated its 50th Anniversary in 1979. Ernest Perriman was club secretary for nearly 25 years, giving up the chairmanship to take over these duties.

The Village House had been a private house, at one time home to the Commandant of the Military Academy at Cowley, and later owned by a Professor Joy. A woman by the name of Kate Lay ran a small cafe next door, in premises which later became part of the Club.

The original Village House.

The rear of the property.

Cowley Workers Club, children's outing to Dudley Zoo in 1961. Over 250 children, between the ages of 9 and 13, were taken on six coaches, all expenses paid by the Cowley Workers Social Club.

Cowley Workers Club, sixth annual pensioners outing in 1962, for a total of 104 Cowley Works pensioners.

The Glee Singers

The Party, as the original group of Welsh Singers called themselves, originated informally at the Cape of Good Hope in 1928 (see *The Changing Faces of Cowley* , Book 2). However, by 1929 the group had expanded and changed its name.

The Rev. Whatley White and the members of the Cowley Congregational Church invited the then Cowley Male Voice Choir to practise on the church premises. Initially they were loaned £1 for music by a Mr Taylor and were led by the church choir conductor, Mr Hardacre.

In 1931 the group changed its name to the Oxford Welsh Prize Glee Singers, but the 'Prize' was dropped soon after. An annual concert was held in St James Hall in Cowley, which continued until 1939; however, it ceased during the war. Many eminent Welsh soloists supported the choir at these events. They competed and were successful in eisteddfods and music festivals throughout the country. In 1938 they came second in the Welsh National Eisteddfod held at Cardiff, in the class for exile choirs.

The choir in 1937. Left to right back row: —, —, —, —, —, Charlie Soper, Eddie —, Haydn Evans. Middle row: Harold Bull, Sid Lewis, Albert Gore, —, Billy Roberts, —, —, —, —, — Williams, Harry Dunkley. Front row: Tom Jones, Ieun Hengoed, Ben Watkins, — Jenkins, Morgan Williams, Roy Hall, Willie Davies (conductor), Roy Wagstaff, Arthur Hayes, Tom Bevan, Moel Roberts, Dorothy Jones.

The choir in July 1948, after winning the Northampton Eisteddfod. They are assembled outside St Christopher's Junior School in Temple Road where they practised during the 1930s and 1940s. Left to right back row: Billy Harris, Bill Roberts, − Jenkins, Billo Roberts, Leslie Brockless, David Richards, Jack Evans, Tom Bevan. Middle row: Tom Jones, −, −, Sid Lewis, Ieun Hengoed, −, −, Moel Roberts, Mr Hughes, − Davies, −. Front row: Harold Bull, Arthur Hayes, Morgan Williams, Eileen Hayes (pianist), Willie Davies (conductor), Harry Dunkley, Walter Davies, Haydn Evans, Tom Richards.

Outside the Swan public house, leaving for a competition at Stratford on Avon in the 1930s.

Rehearsing for a competition at Morris's Clubhouse in Crescent Road, c1950. Group includes, left to right: Harold Bull, Ben Watkins, Arthur Hayes, Sid Lewis, Willie Davies (conductor), Jack Evans, Haydn Evans, Tom Richards, Tom Bevan, Moel Roberts, Walter Davies, Harold Dunkley.

A concert at John Bunyan Baptist Church c1970. Left to right back row: Bernard Maliphant, Tom Jones, –, Arthur Taylor, Haydn Evans, –, Jack Barrett. Middle row: , Neil McColl, –, Haydn Cooper, Jack Evans, Granville Ballinger. Front row: Fred Berry, Arthur Hayes, Eileen Hayes (pianist), Mr Wagstaff, Maurice Fathers, Bill Ward, Moel Roberts, Leslie Brockless.

Top Town Competition 1956. The choir represented Oxford against Newport, Monmouthshire, in the televised final – and won. After a preliminary competition at Abingdon it was reported that 'the evening was stolen by a group that has recently joined the team – the Oxford Welsh Glee Singers – whose unpretentious and unified singing was the most polished performance in the show.' One member of the group remembers singing all the way home, arriving back in Oxford at 4.00 a.m. – but they were all in work in the factory at 7.00 a.m. Left to right: Tom Jones (half in picture), Neil McColl, –, –, Moel Roberts, Granville Ballinger, –, –, Mayor and Mayoress, Harry Dunkley, Harold Bull, Haydn Evans, Arthur Taylor, –, Haydn Cooper, –, –, –, –, Bill Ward, –, –, Leslie Brockless.

The Temple Cowley Ladies Choir seen here c1985. This choir formed in 1934, was originally known as The Women's Own Choir, and continued until 1990. They practised in Temple Cowley United Reformed Church. Left to right back row: Phyllis Cordes, Gwen Summers, Hetty Phillips, Elsie Franklin, Bessie Ramsey, Madge Dexter, –. Front row: Lilian Morley, Bertha Arnold, Daisy Reed, Rosie Boore, Walter Arnott (conductor), Mary Share, Norah Clarke, Nan Arnott, Eileen Hayes (pianist).

Cowley Conservative Club

A group photograph c1950 includes: Bill Simpson, Edith Collis, Lil Bird, R S M Parker, Reg Smith, Edna Smith, Hilda Bennett, Jack Bennett, Mrs Gee, Mrs Mold, Mr Johnson, Mrs Johnson.

Mr S Howard White, senior vice-president of The Cowley Conservative Club presents a clock to Mr Reg Smith, who retired as chairman of the club, after ten years.

The wedding of Una Smith and Gordon Dean on 16 May 1959. The reception was held in the original club in Between Towns Road. Reg Smith, president of the club and father of the bride, makes his speech. Left to right: Trevor Dean, Reg Dean, Edna Smith (president of the Ladies Section), Gordon Dean, Una Smith, Reg Smith, Norah Dean, Jill Tappin.

57

Mr J Mitchell on the right is receiving the Frank Bird Challenge Cup from the club president, Mr Reg Smith, at the Cowley Conservative Club's horticultural show in August 1962.

Mr Jesse Merritt on the left won the Cowley Conservative Club Cup for the best exhibit in show, the cup for the best exhibit in fruit and the Show Cup for the best in flowers. There were a record 390 entries for the 1962 horticultural show.

Jack Bennett with prize dahlias in the 1960s at the annual horticultural show.

Scouts, Guides and Brownies

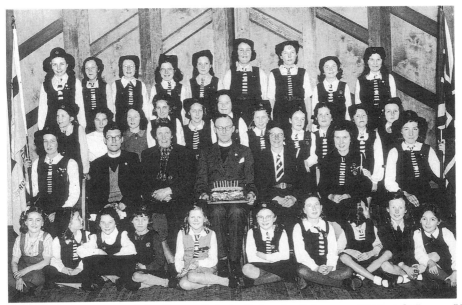

The 9th Birthday Party of the Better Britain Brigade, February 1944 at St James Hall.

The forerunner of the Guiding movement, was the Better Britain Brigade. This company was formed in 1935. The Brigade was the girls section of the Church Army and in 1946 became the 5th Cowley St Luke's Church Army Guides. Left to right, back row: Georgina −, −, −, Valerie Mabbutt, −, −, −, Maureen Kightley, −. Next row: −, Norah Claridge, Ivy Jupp, Mary Bishop, −, June Mabbutt, Rosemary Marshall, Pat Whelan, Valerie Jennings, Shirley Iles, Jean Cooksey. Next row: Jean Durham, Rev. Bolton, −, Rev. Alec Whye, Sister D K Shields, Joan Reid, −. Front row: Anne Trinder, Margaret Marshall, −, −, Anne Edginton, Sheila Kelly, Fay Emanuel, −, Mollie −, −.

The 4th Cowley Brownies in August 1940. Middle row: sixth from left Elizabeth Fussell, and eighth from left Maureen Chatterton.

The 3rd Cowley Brownies c1976. Left to right back row standing: Claire Hanlon, –, Helen Weston, Joanne Emberton, Kate Spencer, Anita–, Wendy Perks. Seated: Ginny Stroud, Donna Jacobs, Mrs Smith, Kay Drake, Lorraine Mills, Carol Hanlon. Front row: Paula Bennett, Jennifer Toomey, Kay–, –, Alison Crocker, Natalie Williams, Louise Gardner.

The 25th Oxford (Salesian Oratory) c1937. Left to right back row: Francis Roche, Francis Howlett, Peter Busby, –Gingell, Fred Ellis, Bill Gleeson, Bill Church, Tommy Gleeson, Roger Bennett, Ernest Wright. Next row: Fred Bennett, Maurice McAvoy, Smith, Frank Blackwell, Denis Cantell, Tony Large. Seated: Denis Colman, Paul Baker, George Robinson, Father Anderon SDB, Ted Burke, Bro. John Vanston SDB, Lawrie Church, Peter Baker, Tony Hancock. In front: Patrick Roche, Phil Powley, Reg Enright, Raymond Paddon, John East, Robert Chambers, Billy McMain.

Schools

Elmthorpe Convent and Our Ladies School

Elmthorpe Convent in 1999 with Sister Anne Darwin, the retiring head teacher of Our Lady's First School.

Elmthorpe House (the central section of the building) was built by William Morris c1920. However, it is alleged that his wife disliked being close to the factory, so the house was sold to the Salesian Sisters in 1924 for a novitiate, a place of preparation for novices who were preparing for work overseas, particularly in Africa. It is now used as a home for the sick and aged and has been extensively extended.

The Salesian Sisters started a school in Elmthorpe House soon after their arrival, but numbers grew and Our Lady's junior mixed and infant school started on 4 April 1932 with Sister Charlotte as head teacher, Miss Ward and 66 pupils. It was officially opened by Doctor Leighton Williams, Archbishop of Birmingham, on 30 April 1932. There appears to have been a nursery class in existence from the early days but this closed in November 1950 due to decreased numbers.

The log book records the admission of evacuees during the war with the influx of 23 in April 1942, which caused overcrowding. School life was frequently disrupted by air raids, visits to the shelters and gas mask inspections.

The School continued to grow and at Sister Charlotte's retirement, after 34 years and 8 months in office, the school roll stood at 260 pupils. The closure of the nursery relieved the pressure on accommodation in the infant department and the building was extended in 1957 as the school celebrated its Silver Jubilee. It became a first school on 3 September 1974.

Our Lady's Nursery School, Christmas 1945. Left to right, back row: Sister Mary, Sally Walsh (helper), Kevin Mullahy, –, Ed Bloyce, Harry Good, –, –, John Moriarty, Pete Gallatly, Sister –?, Mrs Renshawe (helper). Third row: Mick Willoughby, John Creed, Dave Pope, –, –, Mick Walsh, Paul Breen, Mick Rowles, –. Second row: –, –, Danny O'Mahony, Jonnie O'Mahony, Jim Smith, –, –, Muriel McCormack?. Front row: Sheila Meeham?, Maureen Casey, –, –, –, –, –.

The school celebrated its Golden Jubilee in April 1982.

Margaret Batey, the head teacher, is seen on the left with Sister Charlotte, who was invited to cut the cake.

Margaret Batey, head teacher, and Sister Charlotte.

Between 1932 and 1999, the school has only had four head teachers:

Sister Charlotte 1932–1966   Arthur Graham 1967–1973
Margaret Batey 1973–1990   Sister Anne Darwin 1990–1999.

The school staff in 1973, just before Arthur Graham resigned in order to take up the post of Head Teacher at the newly established John Bosco R.C. Middle School in Temple Road. Left to right, back row: Elizabeth Adams, Avis Moriarty, Sr Helen, Monica Wagstaff, Sr Sara, Mrs Beresford-Pierce. Front row: Arthur Graham (head teacher), Kathleen Pill, Sr Pauline, Willa Crow, Maria Hayes, Aeneas McNuity (deputy head).

Arthur Graham had been appointed as deputy head to Sister Charlotte in 1964 and took over the headship at her retirement.

The retirement of Margaret Batey on 20 July 1990. Left to right, back row: Luke Kearney, Sam Edwards, Paul Grant, Margaret Batey (head teacher), Anna-Maria Merola, Denise Kelly, Nicholas Baldwin. Front row: Adele Molyneux, Clarie McManus, Christopher MacDonald, Brigitte McGuinness, Jack O'Sullivan, Samantha O'Donnell.

The Mornese Centre

The centre opened in 1999 on the site of a hall which was built in 1927. The old hall was registered as unsafe in July 1998 and has been replaced. It stands between Elmthorpe Convent and Our Lady's First School and is dedicated to St Mary Mazzarello who was born in Mornese. It is to be used for the benefit of young people and families from all denominations and has the following aims:

> to create a base where young people can gather for recreational and informal educational activities;
> to offer support to parents and families (especially those who are in need); and
> to develop Salesian spirituality among Leaders and young people.

St Christopher's School

St Christopher's School in Temple Road. An aerial view taken in 1989 showing the temporary classrooms at the rear. This site faces that of the original infant and junior schools which were closed c1980. Three classrooms and the hall were opened on this site on 30 March 1966. The building was to be used as an annexe to the main school in Temple Road, and replaced St James Parish Hall, which had housed three classes since 14 September 1936. The building continued as an annexe to the main school until 1980. The numbers dropped after the city reorganisation into the three tier system, and it was no longer viable to maintain the accommodation on both sites. The main school was sold for housing and all children were accommodated on the 'annexe' site.

The original buildings of St Christopher's, taken in 1986 shortly before demolition for the development of St Christopher's Place. Note the air raid shelters in close proximity to the buildings.

Cowley St Christopher's Junior School in September 1967. This was built on the orchard and allotments of Temple Cowley School. (OPA)

Prize winners from Class I in July 1978. Left to right back row: Bernard Durbin head teacher, Rev. Patrick Parry-Okeden, Counc. White, Mrs Smith, Mrs Rumble, Counc. Fred Ingram chairman of the managers. Children left to right: Rebecca Robins, Natalee Williams, Julie Price, Emma Houghton, Sarah Mallett, Dominic Mcaneaney, Andrew Harris.

The opening of the building extensions in March 1996. Left to right back row: Bishop Richard Harris, James Plaskett, Gwen Ranklin. Second row: Kathy Turner (head teacher), Melisa Huntley, Harriet Pearce, Councillor Geoffrey Fowler, Orello Ellis. Front row: Liam Newbold, Natalie Aduma.

St Christopher's war-time allotment. Left to right across the back: G Lusty, D Banton, −, G Keen, −, D Cook. In middle: D Munday, −. In front: −.

St Christopher's Junior School girls swimming team, pictured at Temple Cowley swimming pool in 1952. Left to right: Beryl Simms, Linda Brooks, −, Eileen Swaine, Susanne Slack, Jessica Evans, Jean Bowerman.

Temple Cowley School

War-time allotment at Temple Cowley School. Derek Waterfield is the young lad standing sixth from the left. The head teacher, Herman Munday, is standing in the back row third from left. *'We used to have gardening lessons in the 1950s; our teacher was Spud Taylor.'*

Celebration of Empire Day, 24 May 1950 at Temple Cowley School. Deidre Inns, is in the St John's Ambulance Group.

The Hut School - Cowley St James

Cowley St James Infants School 1948. The infant department was housed in the hut at the top of Beauchamp Lane during the Second World War. It was known locally as The Hut, or Mrs Northway's School. Left to right back row: −, −, Yvonne Instone, − Greta Lamas, −, Wendy Eden, Joan Williams, Maureen Hughes, Mrs Northway. Third row: David Joseph, −, Anthony Cross, Kenneth Platt, Kenneth−, Mike Brogden, −, −, −, Tony Kitchen, Tony Hilsdon, Ian Clamp. Second row: Valerie Clapton, Valerie Webb/Martin?, Elizabeth Barrett, Hazel Evans, Joan Ebbes, Ann Cooke, Rosemary Dowle, −. Front row: Edward Aries, Michael Florey, John Vivian, Richard Emanuel, Peter Brooks, Cedric Davies, −.

The 'hut' at the top of Beauchamp Lane was built c1942 on glebe land as an annexe to Cowley St James School. Numbers had grown with the influx of wartime evacuees and the building housed the infant department in two classrooms until the 1950s. The building continued to be used by the School Meals Service until 1960, when it was offered back to the school. Mrs Rosanne Butler took up the challenge to work there in isolation, occupying one classroom, while the other remained in use as the school canteen.

It ceased to be used by the school in the 1970s. Between 1975 and 1977 it housed Singletree Nursery while the new building was being erected, after which the Hut was used as the church hall. The Playgroup started in the mid 1970s and still thrives.

St James Church Sunday School children with Father Whye in 1947. The children are in fancy dress and are proceeding to the Hut at the top of Beauchamp Lane (formerly Church Street).

The whole group of Sunday School children in the playground of The Hut, after the procession of 1947.

The cast of 'Sleeping Beauty', performed at Christmas 1961 by St James School lower juniors. Left to right, back row: Susan Hills, Elizabeth Grundy, Jacqueline Tapsell, Lynn Mortlock, Anne Scoones. Next row, standing: 'fairy' Patricia French, Susan Bradley, Peter Miles, Ian Grant, Susan Upshall, Graham Martin, Lindie Jenkins, Martin Smith, 'witch' Janice Jackson. Next row, kneeling: Graham Hobbs, Sally Yates, Robert Fuller, Susan Bartlett, Stephen Handley. Seated: Michael Morbey, Stephen McKnight, Shirley Hanlon, Graham Kemp, Isobel Grant.

The same class holding a Christmas Party 1961 inside The Hut school. The teacher on the right is Mrs Butler.

Cowley St James in Beauchamp Lane

The class of top juniors in 1951. Left to right, back row: Kenneth Platt, Tony Hinton, Michael Shrimpton, Roger Stanley, Miss Dyer, Elizabeth Redpath, Janet Marsden, Joan Williams, Angela Cooper. Next row: Cath Bennett, Rosemary Locke, Margaret Smith, Janet Jacobs, Helen Latham, Wendy Evans, Yvonne Inston, Tony Kilbin. Next row: Kathleen Cripps, Anne Cooper, Michael Florey?, Roger Goulder, Kathleen Chick, Anne Brooks, Maureen Hughes. Front row: Michael Brooks, David Hinton, Joy Cooper, Hazel Evans, John Bayliss.

Top Juniors at Hill End Camp 1962. Left to right, back row: −, −, Colin Davies, −, Andrew Hack, Alan Miles, Russell Sharpe. Middle row: Roger Trueman, Brian −, Barry Phipps, Rosanne Butler (teacher), Janet Cattle, Brenda Bartlett. Front row: Judy Bainton, Linda Smith, Elizabeth Ranklin, Helen Butler (baby), Pearl Edwards.

St James School c1939. These girls were all dressed in crepe paper dresses and the group includes: Ruth Truss, Jenny Bryant, Jackie Bebbington, Jack Woods, Marie Pether, Sheila Walton, Jill Woods, Shirley Ward, Rita Whittington, Margaret Smith, Pat Cook, Barbara Ransome, Helen Metcalfe, Audrey Cockrane, June Taylor, Brenda Moss. Margaret Smith went on to become the acress, Dame Maggie Smith.

St James School 1972. Left to right, back row: Basil Foster (head teacher), Paula Smith, Kim Tebbutt, Elizabeth Cooper, Paul Merritt, Stephen Kuht, Tim Smith, Russell Lloyd, Chris Martin, Ricky Turner, Thelma Telling. Middle row: Carlos Lloyd, Antony Lock, Matthew Franklin, Yvonne Jones, Paul Dunckley, Carole Moore, Stephen Harper, Gary Hicks, Caroline Hallett, Ian Williamson. Front row: Bohdan Giduch, June Gregory, Tony Dales, Antony Cooper, Philip Harding, Tracy Turner, Sally Ann Mansell, Brian Gregory.

St James School final year 1974. Left to right, back row: Nicholas Carter, Craig Wright, Jocylin Jones, – Turner, Ricky Turner, David –, –, Anthony Lock, Anthony Cooper, –, Robin Woodford, Ida Nicholls, Christopher Martin, Paul Dunkley. Third row: Andrew Hollis, Neil Tidy, Martin Langford, Ian –, –, –, Melanie Jenkins, Julian Carter, Hugh Williamson, –, Paul Burgess, Richard Mazonowich, Carlos LLoyd, –, Mr Hutchins (lollipop man). Second row: Steven Hallatt, Mrs Merritt, Mrs Tucker, Mr O'Connor, Mrs Harris, Alderman Bromley, Miss Telling, –, Mrs Malony, Mrs Davis, Mrs Cross, Rev Walker, Andrew Edward. Front row: Elizabeth Cooper, Gary Hicks, Kim Wright, Phillip Harding, Russell Lloyd, Yvonne Jones, Steven Koot, Paul Merritt.

Church Cowley Primary School, Bartholomew Road

The first admission of junior aged children to the new building on 22 April 1958.

Church Cowley School, rear view, taken on the first day.

The school opened on 22 April 1958, with 240 pupils. It was built in 13 months at a cost of approximately £40,000. The light, modern classrooms and bright colour schemes, which included red pillars, blue panels, sage green patterned wall paper and natural wood, were greatly admired. The new school catered for infant and junior children between the Garsington Road/Between Towns Road, Rose Hill and the City boundary; these children had previously travelled long distances to both city and county schools.

The school was officially opened by Sir Edward Boyle, Parliamentary-Secretary, Minister of Education, on 4 July 1958. Miss E M Jackson, head teacher, and Mr John Garne, Chief Education Officer, and 120 parents attended a short ceremony in the school hall.

In 1974 the City reorganised into the three-tier system. Consequently numbers dropped in the primary schools and Cowley St James Church of England School in Beauchamp Lane closed. The name of St James, and its status as a C of E Voluntary Controlled School was then transferred to Church Cowley Primary School, which then became Church Cowley St James C of E First School.

Mr Bodenham talks to his class on the first morning

May celebrations 1959. The children proceeded through the school and gardens to welcome in the May. Left to right: Robert Webb, Linda Cox, Christine Room. Solidiers: Kevin Tanner, John Gee, Alan Hewlett, Stephen Purcell. Trumpeters: Stephen Hill, Robert Gardner. Front: Michael Patrick.

Netball team 1960/61. Left to right, back row: P Brown, R Williams, J Hughes, S Simms.
Front row: A Hackett, C Brown, S Holt, P Atherton.

Football team 1960/61. Group includes: — Robinson, S Atherton, R Carter. Middle row:
—, C Wilcox, D Taylor. Front row: S Kilbee, —, K Russell.

The boys of Church Cowley St James School win the Oxford Schools Football Shield in 1975. Left to right back row: Mr D Rigden, Timothy Allen, Justin Broxall, –, Christian Smart, Steven Smart, Christopher Hayes, Richard Reeder, Mr Basil Foster (head teacher). Front row: Michael McCrohen, Anthony Walton, Christopher Hawkins, Mark Purcell, Michael Clarke, Keith Robinson.

The Country Dancers, Summer 1977. Left to right, back row: Karen Lockwood, Cheryl Oliver, Andrea Roberts, Mrs F Wylie, Steven Perks, –, Shirley Carroll, Julie Harvey. Front row: Sharon Brockall, Linda Gotts, –, Nichola Murphy, Ann Marie Pieri, Emma Weston, Donna Weston.

The School celebrates the wedding of Prince Charles and Lady Diana Spencer in 1981. The staff at the back, left to right, includes: Dorothy Kavanagh (deputy head), Pat Dewhurst, Jo Brettell, Barbara Hines, –, –, Helen Gray, Basil Foster (head teacher).

An aerial view over Donnington School in 1958. Opposite the school, to the left, is the Community Centre and to the right the Second World War air raid shelters with the cycle speedway track to the rear. Edmund Campion, later St Augustine's Upper School, can be seen on Iffley Turn to the right of the picture. (OPA)

Donnington School

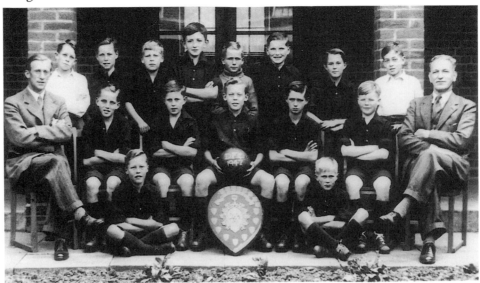

Donnington football team 1947, winners of the Junior School Shield, the final of which was played on the Whitehouse Ground, Abingdon Road, Oxford. Left to right, back row: Malcolm Davies, Pat Gibson, John Allen, Doug Stewart, Terry Foster, D Stewart?, Keith Britnell, Brian Cox. Middle row: Mr Eyles, Brian Gale, Peter Evans, Mick Allen, D 'Goosey' Wetheral?, Brian Davies, Mr Hart (head teacher). In front: R Jones, Brian Munday.

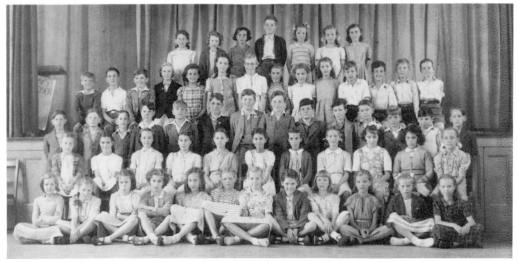

Donnington School c1950. Left to right, back row: Valerie Foster, –, Jocelyn Cox, –, Sheila Parkhouse, Pat –, –. Next row: John Poyser, –, –, –, Alice Earl, Barbara Newbold, Carol –, –, –, Eileen Powell, Colin Ponting, –, –, –. Next row: – Frost, –, –, John Noble, David Bourton, –, –, –, Roland Parker, –, Edward Sherman, David Franks, Malcolm Davies, –. Next row: –, –, –, Anne Richardson, June Taplin, Sheila Dobson, Anne Taylor, Phyllis Guest, –, Brenda Sanders, Hilda Helm. Front row: Joan Elliot, Wendy Miller, –, Dorothy Pauly, Mavis –, Sylvia Boyce, Jean Batts, Pat Harper, Celia Randall, Beryl Clark, –, Wendy Law.

Public Houses

Prince of Wales, Horspath Road

Sid Morley outside the Prince of Wales soon after its completion in 1935.

Sid and Edith Morley, with daughter Rene and son Len, just before moving into the Prince of Wales.

Sid Morley was one of the first employees of William Morris at his Longwall Garage and continued to work for him until trying his hand in the licencing trade. Sid and his wife, Edith, opened for business in November 1935 as the first tenants of the Morrell's owned Prince of Wales, Horspath Road.

At first they only had a beer licence, but in 1937 they acquired the wine and spirits licences previously held by only two other houses.

Sid and Edith ran the Prince of Wales until 1948 when their daughter, Rene, and her husband, Monty Burgess, took over. Rene carried on running the business after Monty's death in 1980, with the help of her son, Terry, before retiring in 1986.

During the war the pub cellar was an ARP Communications Centre and, more recently, was a meeting place for members of the Far East Prisoner of War Association.

Rene and Monty Burgess behind the bar of the Prince of Wales in 1955.

Rene celebrating the first 50 years of the Prince of Wales.

The Prince of Wales bar billiards 'A' and 'B' teams in the 1953/4 season. Left to right: Jimmy Hicky, Alby Lewis, Gordon Blizzard, Harry Jones, Roy Payne, Charlie Mustard (at back), Ken Organ, Monty Burgess, Vic Thorne, Alan Organ, Gil Organ. Ken and Alan Organ, Gordon Blizzard and Harry Jones went on to become Oxford Individual Champions.

The Ladies Darts team, section winners of 1965. Left to right: Pam Ball, Gwen Pendry, Rene Burgess, Grace Padbury, Norma Whiting, Molly Taylor.

Exeter Hall, Oxford Road

Richard Lee became landlord of the Exeter Hall in 1894 and ran the public house until his death in 1916. His wife, Mary Jane (nee Hall) took over from her husband until her own death in 1928.

The Lee family c1912. Left to right, back row: Harold, Ivy, Richard, Aunt?, William. Seated: Richard Lee, Mary Jane Lee. Front row: Alf, Gladys, Ducker.

The Exeter Hall was the meeting place for the Ancient Order of Britons (Loyal Marsh Lodge) and the Royal Antediluvian Order of Buffaloes (Morris Cowley Lodge).

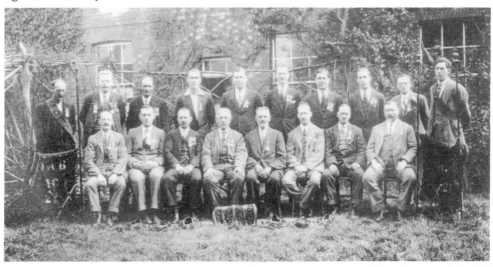

Group of Royal Antediluvian Order of Buffaloes, in the garden of the Exeter Hall c1923.

Business and Occupation

Cowley Centre to Templars Square

The Development Plan of 1955 stated the intention of the Oxford City Council to *'provide a business and shopping centre at Cowley to meet the increasing needs of the population to the south east of the city, and in so doing to relieve some of the existing congestion of the old City.'*

The area required to accommodate the new Cowley Centre was estimated at some twenty-three acres, and the land was accordingly designated for compulsory purchase in March 1953. The Compulsory Purchase Order was finally confirmed in June 1957, listing sixty-nine existing dwellings and thirty-six retail or business premises containing a further twenty-six dwellings. All buildings within the area covered by the Order were to be demolished, with the exception of the Nelson public house, which was to be integrated into the new Plan.

The Cowley Centre Committee was set up in February 1958 to steer the future development. They faced many difficult decisions, not least was the fact that *'we were changing an area which was a backwater, partly derelict, partly industrial and partly quiet suburban residential into a town centre. There were many personal problems of families and businesses displaced, of the amenities of people's lives severely encroached upon, in some cases permanently.'* The Cowley Community Association, itself mainly housed in derelict premises, became the local focus point, where the people of Cowley could be consulted and kept advised of these rapid, and drastic, changes to their way of life.

The first work began on site in July 1960, being the diversion of Hockmore Street and Between Towns Road, and the first shop to open was Fine Fare Supermarket in June 1962.

Two multi-storey car parks were built, the first, in Hockmore Street, was started on 9 November 1960, completed on 1 August 1962, to hold 350 cars at a cost of £250 per car parking space. The second car park, in Crowell Road, was possibly the most controversial of the building development. This was begun on 12 August 1963 and completed on 11 February 1965, and the cost was greater, at £400 per car parking space.

For five years the people of Cowley had endured the insistent noise of drills and pile drivers, diverted roads and seas of mud, but the dream of Cowley Centre was finally realised.

List of Traders in 1965.

Radio Rentals	Co-Operative Society
Cadena Cafe	London Kiosks Newsagents
Southern Electric	Cut Cost Cleaning
Relay Exchange	Chiltern Drycleaners
Robert Stanley Opticians	Oxford Fruit and Flower Co
Rayburn Menswear	Peterwood Lingerie
Montague Burton Menswear	Currys Ltd
Trueform Shoes	John Collier Menswear
Fine Fare	Southern Gas
H P Tyler	Contessa Lingerie
Bata Shoes	Etam Ladies Fashion
Webbers Dept. Store	Baxters Butchers
International Supermarket	McFisheries
Shergolds Ironmongers	Wallpaper Stores
Faringdon Shoes	Bollom Ltd
Will R Rose Photographers	Parslows Bakers
Advance Laundries	Harrison & Clarke Chemists
Beryl Morris Hairdresser	Colorbrush
Lyons & Lyons	Sketchleys
John Temple Menswear	Lewis Separates
Meredith Shoes	Foster Bros Menswear
Hilton & Sons Shoes	James Walker Jewellers
Dorothy Perkins	Van Allen Ladies Fashions
Atkinson Television	Wyeths Ltd Cycles
Anstey Opticians	Modern Shoe Repairs
Percy Lewis Bookmakers	Jones & Co Wines
Sainsburys	F W Woolworths
W H Smith	Wards Furniture and Fabrics
Morgan Bakers	D Goodwin Menswear
Television Services	Batemans Opticians
Leech & Hainge Electrical	Freeman Sports Goods
Seagull Laundrette	W & S Supplies
Barclays Bank	Lloyds Bank
White Rabbit Snack Bar	The Lewis Carroll Restaurant

Cowley Centre was officially opened on 21 May 1965 by Richard Crossman, Minister of Housing, accompanied by the Lord Mayor of Oxford, Alderman J N L Baker and Mrs Baker. The main contractors had been John Laing Construction Limited, and the total estimated cost was £1.4 million.

The fountain in the Main Square, seen here in the 1960s, was a major feature of the new Cowley Centre. Over the years it became very dilapidated and abused and was finally removed during reconstruction of the Main Square and Pound Way. The development on the right hand side shows Sainsburys being built.

The Main Square of Cowley Centre has always been used for various promotions. This event, entitled the Moon Ride Cycle, could be seen during August 1970.

The White Rabbit Snack Bar and The Lewis Carroll Restaurant were opened by Easter 1965. They occupied the first three floors of Pound House, a six storey block at the west end of Cowley Centre overlooking the Banking Court. The self-service snack bar could seat up to eighty people and was entered directly from the Banking Court. The Restaurant included waitress service and was approached by way of an external staircase, seen here on the left hand side, with a terrace running round two sides of the building.

The new Between Towns Road, the first part of the Cowley Centre scheme to be completed, opened to traffic on 11 September 1961. *'Shortly after 10.00 a.m. Mr R W Baker, the reisdent engineer for Oxford Corporation, and his men removed their improvised pipe-and-plank barriers from each end of the new road and transferred them to Hockmore Street, which it replaces. Some of the drivers of vehicles coming from Knolles Road towards Cowley Road overlooked the Keep Left signs on the new roundabout at the eastern end and cut round to the right. At the other end vehicles from Crowell Road cut the corner into the new road until a temporary island was placed in position. There is an awkward junction here, because the Council cannot align the road properly until numbers 58 and 60 Hockmore Street come into its possession and can be pulled down.'* (Report from *The Oxford Mail* .)

The mini roundabout at the junction of Between Towns Road and Barns Road, July 1978.

Between Towns Road as it was in 1958. The first photograph looks past the old Nelson along Hockmore Street, the second, taken from the same viewpoint, is the opposite direction along Between Towns Road towards the Swan. The houses are on the site of the present day Sainsbury store.

BETWEEN TOWNS ROAD,
Cowley.
From 182 Oxford road to Hockmore street. Map H 9.
South-east side.
2 Drake Mrs
2 Advance Laundries (A. L. (Oxford) Ltd.) (receiving office)
4 Orsborn Wltr. fried fish shop
6 **EDGINTON'S OF COWLEY,** hardware dlrs. & ironmongers, paint & wallpaper specialists, tools, fireplaces & oil heating. Tel. Oxford 77402
6A, Northfield Cecil H
8 **EDGINTON C. & G.** children's outfitters, drapers, wools & ny.ons. Tel. 77402
10 Bollom Ltd. dyers & cleaners
12 Ownsworth Jn. shopkpr
12 Howes Terence
14 **COWLEY FURNISHERS,** house furnishers. Telephone, Oxford 78560
16 & 18 Durham A. & Son, fruitrs

20 Lainsbury Miss
23 **WHITE J. J.** plumber, gas & hot water fitter. Tel. Oxford 77210
24 Watts F. R. butcher
24A, **MORRIS & BEECHAM'S FUEL SERVICE** (G. H. J. Morris), coal merchants. Telephone, Oxford 77148
St. James' Church Hall
28 Noke Geo
30 Cook Geo. D
30 Holton Rt. E. confctnr
32A, Clements Wm
32B, Hackett Mrs. C
32 Holton Rt. Donald
34 Woodward Misses
38 & 40 Oxford & District Co-operative Society Ltd
..... here is St. Omer rd .....
42 Agutter Hy. Jas. grocer
42 Gibbons Wltr. T. baker
44 Phillips Bertie
46 Bacon Ronald
48 Smith Miss M
50 Kent Harry
52 Johnson Miss A
54 Agutter Hy. J. café
58 Smith & Low, wireless dlrs
60 Goodman Hubert
60 Taylor H. J. & Sons Ltd. bldrs

62 Willis Fredk. Jn
64 Brooks Wltr. C
66 Bowerman Mrs
68 Baston Leonard Geo
70 Taylor Arth
74 Adams Albt. G
76 East Chas. H
78 Pocock Arth
80 Boardman Albt
82 King Albt. Rt
.....here is Hockmore st......
North-west side
SWAN GARAGE (OXFORD) LTD. ROOTES GROUP STANDARD & TRIUMPH SERVICE AGENTS, motor engnrs. T N Oxford 77054
1 Butler A. & Co. Ltd grocers
3 Bowen Jn. W. hairdrssr
17 **MORGAN G.** commission agent. Tel. Oxford 77652/3 & 78686
17A, Gardiner Harold
17A, Henry B. J. Ltd. motor car delivery agts
19 Cowley Conservative Club
... here is St. Luke's rd ...
43 Johnson Stephen

45 Rutter Arth
47 Bovington Mrs
47 Skilton B. greengro
49 **Tyrer Albt.** grocer & confectionery
..... here is Knolles rd ......
53 **WEL SHOD LTD.** boot repairing contractors (registered office). Telephone No. Oxford 77978
53A, Alder Jas
55 & 59 **CARAVAN & CAR SALES (OXFORD) LTD.** new & second-hand caravan agents & dlrs.; hire purchase arranged on private transactions. Tel. 77380
55 & 59 **CAMBRIA HOUSE FINANCE CO. LTD.** finance agents; hire purchase arranged on private transactions; dealers' enquiries invited (branch address). Tel. 77380
61 Bowman Jas. S
65 Hart Peter M
67 Williams Harold E., M.B.E
69 Jackson Bert
71 Baker Regnld
73 Evans Rt. H
75 Bentley Cecil Harry
...here is Hockmore st......

Kelly's Directory showing residents and businesses in Between Towns Road in 1958 (Reed Information Service)

John Allen & Sons (Oxford) Ltd

The site of this factory, and its extensive grounds, has now been developed into a shopping complex (the John Allen Centre) commemorating one of the most important companies within Cowley.

The original company on this site was established in 1868 and was known as the Oxfordshire Steam Ploughing Company, later the Oxford Steam Plough Company Limited. John Allen bought the business from the Eddison family for £13,000 in 1897, and his two sons, G W G Allen MC and Capt J J Cullimore Allen, joined the firm in 1919. On 1 January 1925 the company changed its name to John Allen & Sons (Oxford) Limited. In the 1970s the company became Grove Allen, later Grove Cranes and the works finally closed in 1984.

A company promotional leaflet of the 1950s stated: *'the total area of these Works, including the Employees' Sports Field, is over ten acres; the area of the Factory Building being over 100,000 square feet. In addition we own our own Gravel Pits, which cover some thirty acres, and also a considerable number of houses which are tenanted by our employees. In our Factory at Cowley we have in operation over one hundred and thirty modern machine tools, all of which are driven by self-contained electric motors'.*

In 1937 the idea of a sports club was first conceived by two members of the office staff, Jimmy Holmes and Lionel Hayward. They called a meeting in the canteen and a cricket club was formed, which gradually evolved into Allen's Sports Club. At first matches were played on a municipal ground at Cowley Marsh, but in 1938 Captain Allen conceived the idea of levelling part of the land for cricket and football grounds. During the Second World War part of this sports field became allotments in response to the Government's 'Grow More Food' campaign. Early members of this sports club included D Wilson, Tom Morriss, E Salter and Ted Meredith. P E Greening was a keen supporter and was responsible for drawing up the

Lionel Hayward at a Sports Day during the early 1940s.

first set of rules. In 1945 the directors gave the club permission to use the canteen during the evenings as a clubhouse and the club was, therefore, registered and able to open its own bar. A fine new clubhouse, adjoining the sports ground, was officially opened on 27 January 1950. The sports club provided facilities for football, cricket, tennis, fishing and motoring, plus indoor activities and annual competitions for the Anderson Darts Cup, the John Allen Snooker Cup, and the Stanley Sears Billiard Cup.

A group of John Allen employees, in the 1930s. John Slack on the left.

A company outing in 1938. Left to right, back row: –, –, John Slack, –, –, Harry Beckett. Front row: –, Ivor Hicks, Clive Anderson.

A tug-of-war event held on the sports field. Stan Goddard in the centre.

Christmas celebrations at John Allen's c1950. Left to right: Amy Scott, Ted Poole, June Chasney, John Scott, Nancy Newling, Dudley Newling.

It was customary for the directors to serve all employees with drinks at Christmas. Left to right: – Patterson, Cynthia Poore, –, –, Arthur Anderson (managing director), –, Phillip Caudwell, Cyril Wiggins, Bob Shepherd, –, June Chasney, Dudley Newling, Phil Harvey (behind), Dorothy Kent. Bob Shepherd is remembered as smoking an extraordinary large pipe, and this can be seen in this photograph of c1951.

A '25 year' Dinner in the late 1950s. Left to right standing: Fred Hale, Geoff Launchbury, Capt. Cullimore Allen, Arthur Anderson (managing director), Arthur Pollard (works manager). Seated: Dudley Newling, Phillip Caudwell, Herbert Rowles, , —. Front seated: Fred Stead, Cyril Wiggins, Jimmy Holmes.

A '25 year' dinner from 1967. Left to right: Len Gee, Peter Smith, John Symes and Maurice Allen.

Staff group c1949. Left to right, back row: Fred Hale, Dudley Newling, Jack Harrison, 'Raggy' Allen, Ken Thomas, Herb Rowles, John Berry, Peter Bampton, Jimmy Holmes, −, − Shayler. Front row: −, − Berry, Clive Anderson, John Anderson, Fred Stead.

John Allen football team 1946. Left to right, back row: J Drake, J Hollier, F Higgins, H Allen, H Fry, A Cassidy, W Houlton, R Curnow, T Thornill, T Morris. Front row: A Rowles, R Thomas, K Poulter, C Willmott, F Bennett.

The retirement of John Slack in 1974. Mr Slack had been with the company since 1933 and worked on the Allen Motor Scythe for many years.

John Allen's Staff in 1954

Accountancy Section:	H F Rogers, S Smith, L Hayward, C Claridge, G Walker, J Harrison, P Osborn, D Hessey.
Cashier:	C M Hawtin.
Correspondence Office:	Mrs E P Fogarty, Mrs J M Poole, Mrs A Scott, Miss N Stoyle, Miss M Farnell, Miss P Walker, Miss A Gardner, Miss B Watts.
Design/Drawing Office:	G Harley, L Carter, H Warner, E Milliard, G W Potts, D B Jocelyn, Mrs E M Jackson, Miss J A Robins, Mrs S Copp.
Receptionist:	Miss S Leach.
Export:	K Thomas, L Ryan, D W Dykes, P J Harte, Mrs J Hyde.
Excavator Sales:	S L McKay, D Newling.
Excavator Orders:	R H Rogers, T Sheppard, P Harvey, P Bampton, F Ingram.
Haulage and Gravel:	G W Smith.
Purchasing:	J T Symes, J Paterson, D Hawtin, Miss J Brockhouse.
Publicity:	J Holmes, C W Wiggins.
Scythe Sales/Technical:	P G Caudwell, J Slack, G Scofield, R A Purdy, H Beckett.
Scythe Order/Despatch:	G Hitchcox, F Rovery, G Whareham, G Robbins, Miss M Uzzell, Miss S Davies.
Works:	A Pollard (Works Manager), W F J Hale (Deputy Works Manager), H Rowles (Superintendent Heavy Erecting Shop), C Anderson (Superintendent Light Erecting Shop), L Shaylor (Superintendent Machine Shop), G D Baker (Foreman Carpenter's Shop), A Hollier (Foreman Boiler Shop), E Dowling (Foreman Paint Shop), M Allen (Head Storekeeper, Heavy and Excavator Stores), J Drake (Motor Scythe Despatch Stores), L Weston (Motor Scythe Production Stores), A D Clarke, W Meades, A A J Wise, R Willis (Progress), J Berry (time keeper), W H Phillips (First Aid Superintendent).

Albert Edward Gray (Carpenter, Undertaker and Coachbuilder).

Left to right: James 'Bert' Gray, Reginald Gray and Albert Gray with two specially commissioned vehicles c1920, seen here at the rear of their premises at 12 Oxford Road.

Albert Edward Gray was born in 1868 at Pembroke Street, now Rectory Road, the son of Matthew Gray, builder. Like most of his family he worked in the carpentry and building trade and for many years was employed by Organ Bros. in Randolph Street, East Oxford.

He finally set himself up in business and in 1911 he moved to 12 Oxford Road, Cowley, on the corner of George Street, now Hendred Street. From here he ran his own carpentry and building business and was also one of the local undertakers. He was also involved in the early years of the motor industry as a coachbuilder, along with his sons, Reginald and James.

In 1926 he died suddenly at the age of 57, and was buried in Rose Hill cemetery. The property was taken over by Eli Smart, undertaker.

E. SMART & SON

Undertakers. Complete Funeral Furnishers

TOWN OR COUNTRY.

Telephone 7072.

12 OXFORD ROAD, COWLEY, OXFORD

An Eli Smart advertisement.

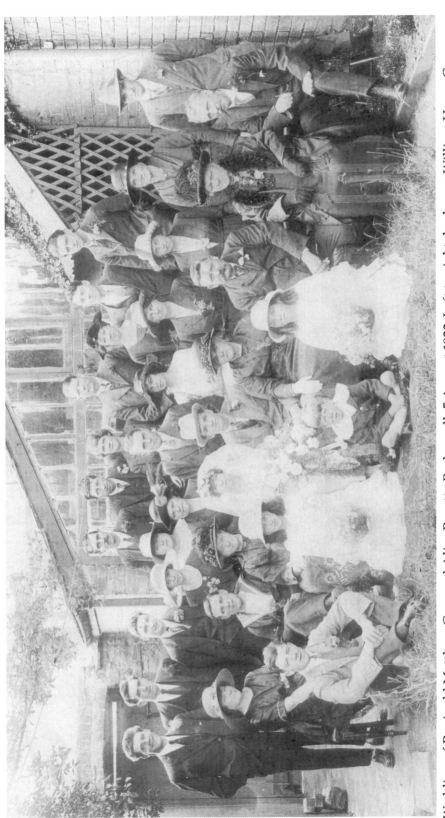

Wedding of Reginald Matthew Gray and Alice Rosetta Beckensall, 5 August 1922. Left to right, back row: William Henry Gray, –, –, George Harry Moss, Flo Wittridge, Edgar Wittridge, –. Standing: Fred Palmer, –, –, Maud Alice Beckensall, Nellie Gray, –, Percy Roberts Kitchener Gray, Winifred Alice Gray, Dorothy Fanny Gray, Eva Agnes Gray, Emily Gray?, 'Bert' James Albert Gray. Sitting: May Palmer, Charles George 'Baden' Beckensall, Emily Margaret Beckensall, Alice Rosetta Beckensall, Reginald Mathew Gray, Mary Ann Gray, Albert Edward Gray, 'Granny' Merrit, –. In front: –, Dora Beckensall, –, Gwendoline Mary Gray.

Wilkins Road

The Springford Dairy, (known locally as Cross's Dairy), 91 Wilkins Road

Ernest Cross ran a dairy off Walton Street in Oxford before coming to the Sunnyside Estate in Cowley to open the Springford Dairy in 1933. Ernest and his wife, Olive (formerly Miss Rogers, head of Cuddesdon School) not only ran the milk round, which covered Cowley from Littlemore Road to Cranmer Road, plus the Lye Valley Estate, they also provided the local factory workers with mid-day meals in their cafe facility.

Cross's ice cream was popular with local children and was served from a window hatch at the front of the shop. Olive Cross, with their ice cream van, was a familiar sight around the streets of Cowley and during the hot summer months 'penny' lollies were the order of the day from children on their way home from school.

Ernest Cross also had an orchard at the end of Oliver Road, now taken over by the Eastern By-pass, which was also well known by the local children. The dairy finally closed in 1953. The premises were occupied by various businesses, including an antique shop and a fishmongers, and are currently shoe menders.

Ernest Cross

Olive Cross

Wilkins Road Post Office and Newsagents c1939, run by H V Hands. Pauline Hands is standing second left. This newsagents was sold to Mr and Mrs Sneddon, who in turn sold to Mr Robinson. The premises have now been absorbed into the extended Spar shop.

Mr Cross and his son, Ron, seen outside Milton's, the hairdressing shop in Wilkins Road. This shop was owned by Mr Milton Wilson.

The Spar shop at 97 Wilkins Road, on the corner of Fernhill Road, in 1986.

Ray and Joyce Titchell ran this corner shop from July 1967 until retirement in May 1988. They took over from Jack and Molly Warren. It was originally a Wavey Line shop, then Mace, finally Spar. Ray and Joyce were well known for their home-made wines, and were regional home-made wine judges.

WILKINS ROAD.

Cowley.
From 12 Horspath road to
37 Fern Hill road
Map I 8, I 9.
South-east side.

2 Archer Cecil E
4 Morris Fras. Wm
6 Cunningham Wm. Jn
8 Edmunds Percy Wilfred
10 Long Geo. Jn
12 Poyner Wm
14 Yeatman Percy Fredk
16 McDougall Rt
18 Tipler Wm. Earls
20 Pipkin Kenneth
22 Merritt Donald
24 Tompkins Rd
26 Page Albt. N
28 Barlow Jn. A
30 Grant Fredk. J
32 Slaughter Norman W
34 Beames Jas
36 Turner Geo. Fredk
38 Ray Mrs. F
40 Burt Jn. Tom
42 Tansley Herbt. Frank
44 Rollings Regnld. Geo
46 Smith Melvyn G
..... here is Marshall rd......

48 Trotman Harry
50 Davies Ormond D
52 O'Connor Frank Edwd
54 Downey Percy
56 Bishop Ronald Thos
58 Robinson Arth. A
60 Shorter Jim
62 Stockford Mrs. D
64 Clark Albt
66 Shuter Mrs. R
..... here is Bleache pl ......
68 Sargent Kenneth
70 Marshall Herbt
72 Wood Andrew
74 Fogden Keith F
76 Hanlon Roy
78 Pudner Regnld. H
80 Harvey Mrs. H. E
82 Cooper Mrs. E. H. D
84 Bates Geo. H
86 Harris Frank
88 Sykes Fredk. K. J
90 Whiteside Mrs

North-west side.

1 Church Arth
3 Chambers Hugh W
5 Jones Wm. Alfd
7 Woods Hy. E
9 Jones Miss E. M
11 Cousins Mrs. E
13 Mills Jn. Wm
15 Dean Thos

17 Johnson Edwd
19 Gibbs Fredk
21 Alford Thos
23 Wootton Albt
25 Llewellyn Wm
27 Thorpe Arth. H
29 Crump Edwin Alfd
31 Wood Albt. Victor
33 Walton Harold
35 Dexter Lambert
37 Farr Maurice E
39 Eakley Edwd. W
41 Cheney Frank H
41 Pope Mrs
43 Buckingham Alfd. Jas
45 Watts Eli
..... here is Marshall rd .....
47 Fleetwood Wm. Albt
49 Williams Fredk
51 Morris Lionel J
53 Burgess Albt. Jn
55 Whittington Geo
57 Proberts Albt. F
59 Cunnington Fredk. H
61 Fletcher Mrs
63
65 Killick Mrs
67 Jaunitis Janis
69 Johnson Wm. F
71 Kilfoil Geo. Albt
73 Cadle Rd
.... here is Oliver rd ....

75 Henderson Philip
75 Davidson Arth. J. chemist
77 Knowlman P. grocer &
  provision merchant.
  Tel. Oxford 77671
79 Hinton F. W. grocer
79 Hinton Fredk. W
81 Palmer Jn. fruiterer &
  florist. Tel. 77865
83 Titcomb Ernest D.
  ladies' outfitter. Tel.
  Oxford 77918
83 Titcomb Ernest D
85 Williams R. J. & H. F.
  grocer & provision
  merchants. Tel. Ox-
  ford 77660
85 Williams Regnld. J
87 Tucker Mrs. P. J. wool
  stores
87 Tucker Jn. H. boot repr
89 Wilson M. H. hairdrssr
89A. Regal Press, printers
91 Nutley Thos. H. fish-
  monger
93 Allmond K. & Co. (Cow-
  ley) Ltd. butchers
93 Jones Roy
95 Taylor David
95 Hathaway J. C. news-
  agent
97 Warren Jack, shopkpr

Wilkins Road 1960 (by kind permission of Reed Information Service).

OXFORD ROAD.

Cowley.
Continuation of Cowley road
to Garsington road.
Map H 9.

South-west side.

2 Stockford Gordon
4 Kernahan Ivan M. motor
  car dlr
8 George Thos. W
10 Hayes Ralph
12 Oxford & District Co-
  operative Society Ltd
  funeral directors
12 Draycott Raymond
..... here is Hendred st .....
14 Dwyer Mrs. E
16 Hengood Mrs. M. F
18 Bowell Mrs. G
20 Browning Mrs. A
22 ... Mrs. V
24 Trafford Arth. Fredk
26 Williams Trevor
28 Dyer Mrs. A. M
30 Pinkney Jas. shopkpr
30 Sadler Alan J
..... here is Littlehay rd .....
32 Grace Fredk. Geo
32A. Royal Liver Friendly
  Society (L. Griffin,
  dist. mangr.). Tel.
  Oxford 78029
34 Castle Mrs
36 Knight Steven E
38 Johnson Chas
44 Merritt Gilbt
46 Law E. E. boot mkr
48 & 50 Bates A. F. Ltd.
  motor engnrs
..... here is Edmund rd .....
52 Wells Geo
52 Wells Mrs. G. wool stores
  & hosier. Telephone,
  Oxford 77939
54 Oakley Mrs
56 Aries Mrs
..... here is Clive rd .....
126 Alder F. & Son, news-
  agents, tobacconists,
  stationers, greeting
  cards & confectionery
  Telephone, Oxford 77255

128 Hobbs G. & C. butchers
130 Home & Colonial Stores
  (H. & C. (Retail) Ltd)
132 EDEN G. W. & SON,
  greengrocers. Tel. Ox-
  ford 77332
134 Westminster Bank Ltd.
  (H. T. Foster, mana-
  ger)
136 Jubilee Lending
  Library (E. E.
  Coates, propr.), sta-
  tioners, tobcconsts, con-
  fectioners, toy dlrs. &
  post office. Tel. Ox-
  ford 77661
138 Freefields, florists
..... here is Havelock rd .....
140 Hills Mrs. S
140 White W. J. P., L.D.S.
  E.Durh. dental surgn
142 & 144 Oxford & District
  Co-operative Society
  Ltd. drapers
144A. Moss Geo
146 Scroggs Harold Edwd.
  dairyman
148
148A. De-la-Fuente David
148A. Davic Equipment Ltd.
  sewing machine reprs
150 MEREDITHS (H. J.
  Bryant, propr.), out-
  fitters. Tel. Oxford
  77023
150 Alwingier Rd
152 Stroek C. A. confec-
  tioner, grocer & tobac-
  conist. Tel. 77301
154 OXFORD TRUS-
  TEE SAVINGS
  BANK (A. G. Palmer
  B.A. general mana-
  ger). Tel. Oxford 77904
..... here is Cleveland drive ...
156 Webb Jn. E. butcher
158 Rose Geo. B. chemist
158 Canning Hubert Jn
160
162 Allport Mrs
164 Firth & Medalia, phy-
  sicians & surgns

161 Firth Edwd. K. A
166 Barclays Bank Ltd. (H
  Hudson, manager)
Hudson Hy. (Bank ho)
170 Tompkins Archn Jas
170 Soames Geo. Hy
176 Giblons Jn. Evelyn
178 DUNFORD D. & SON,
  high-class butcher.
  Tel. Oxford 78381
180 Silk's Stores, grocers
182 Merediths (H. J. Bryant,
  propr.), boot dlrs
184 Beechey W. F. baby
  carriage dlr
186 COWLEY WORKERS'
  SOCIAL CLUB (affili-
  ated to the C. & L. U.)
  (Ernest Perryman,
  sec.; Jn. Davis,
  steward) (The Village
  ho.). Tel. 77132
..here is Between Towns rd..
Original Swan Hotel
Roman Catholic Primary
  School (Our Lady) (junior
  mixed & infants)
Elmthorpe Convent (Rev.
  Sister Superior)

North-east side.

..... here is Marsh rd ......
Exeter Hall P.H
3 Phillips Noel
5 Brooks Ernest
7 Eccles Cyril F
9 Hamblin Wilfred
11 Boswell Harold
13 Fraser Malcolm
15 Willis Mrs. E. greengro
17 Yerbury Sidney K
19 Cook Geo. V
21 Keep Mrs. E
23 Smart Stanley
25 Sims P. & J. grocers &
  provsn. mers. Tel.
  77802
25 Sims Peter
27 Norris Wm. B
29 Roberts Wm. Hy
31 Lee Miss
33 Kirby Ernest
35 Rosser Mrs. D

37 Evelyn, ladies' hair-
  dresser. Tel. Oxford
  77914
37 SPENCER CYRIL, up-
  holsterer (general re-
  pairs). Tel. Oxford
  77907
37A. East H. G. & Co.
  scientific instrument
  mkrs
37A. Morris Fredk. J. decrtr.
  (workshop)
37B. Hodge Cyril G
Emmanuel Hall
39 Leemans Abraham
39A. Hedge Rt. Chas. &
  Sons, carpntrs. (works)
41 Thirtle Bernard
43 Evans Thos. J
45 Spiller Mrs
47 Malin R. J
49 MALINS MOTORS
  (COWLEY) LTD.
  (garage, cars for sale
  & self drive hire;
  repairs). Tel. Oxford
  77573
49 Malin R. & Co. builders.
  Tel. Oxford 77579
51 Mitchell Chas. E
53 Hedge Rt. Chas. & Sons,
  carpntrs
53 Hedge Rt. C
55 Moore Regnld. W
57 Shaw Horace
59 Parsons Jn
61 Yeates Cyril Jsph
63 Brandish Mrs
65 Painter Mrs. M
67 Williams Mrs
69 Keene Mrs
71 Justice Frank

73 Read Chas. Rt
75 Rivers Gerald. decrtr
77 Simpson Matthew
79 Stritch Thos. S
81 Barney Victor Chas
83 Upstone Wm. J
85 Robinson Edwd. Wm
87 Aris Mrs. E
89 Bryan Hy. Cecil F
91 Cruickshank Mrs. N
93
95 Grant W. J. radio engnr

97 Carter Mrs. Alice, shop-
  keeper
99 Page Jn. M
99 Swell Frank, high-class
  boot & shoe repairer
Organ E. & Son, bldrs.
  (yard)
101
111 Dela B
113 Hartley Rt
115 Hartland Harry
115 Hartland H. & Son,
  carpntrs
117 Browne Jn
119 Clark Mrs. A. M
121 Tomkins Fredk. Jn
123 Alexander Thos. Jas
125 Bishop Clifford Jas
127 King Mrs
129 Popple Kenneth J
131A. Cope Bert
131 Red Rose Restaurant
133 MULLETT H. A.
  hairdresser (men's
  stylist). Tel. 77578
133A. Milner H. A
135 Allaway Herbt. Cecil
137 Alder Peter A
139 Smythe Chas. Hewit
143 Butler Sydney
145 Strange Cecil G
147 Gatfield Wm. H
149 Lee Geo
151 Ellis Frank Wm
153 Bunting Mrs
155 Walker Chas. Thos
157 Wines Leonard
159 Witney Wm. Hy
161 Dartnell Chas. Edwd
163 Cooper Arth. Jn
165 Pincington Fred M
167
167A. Siggery Mield. A
169 Cleaver Regnld
Temple Cowley Congre-
  gational Church
..... here is Temple rd .....
St. Luke's Church
..... here is Hollow way .....

Oxford Road, 1960 (by kind permission of Reed Information Service).

Oxford Road

Cullen's Store, 30 Oxford Road, Cowley. Harry Cullen, builder and market gardener, of Garsington, was the owner of Cullen's Store, at the junction with West Street, now Littlehay Road. The shop was run by his daughter, Lizzie Cullen, pictured outside the shop, from 1925 to 1955.

Oxford Road, Cowley 1959. This parade of shops featured in a Christmas feature in the local press promoting the joys of shopping outside the busy City Centre. This was, of course, in the days before the development of Cowley Centre, and these local shops supplied many of the needs of the local community. Merediths, the tailor and gentlemen's outfitters, boasted a *'shop front of blue and grey tiles, mahogany and a perspex facia. Ties are available from 5sh. woollen scarves from 7sh 6d and imitation silk scarves at 10sh 6d. Camel coats are selling at £5 19s 6d and Harris tweed suits are available.'* The proprietor at this time was Mr H J Bryant who also ran Meredith's shoe shop a few doors away. Freefields florists, run by Mr W H Gatfield, had recently moved from premises a few doors away into a larger shop.

Personalities

Ken Halsey

Ken was born in Wellington Street, Jericho in 1913. He attended school at St Barnabas and Oxford High Street for Boys, before going for teacher training at Culham College between 1932 and 1934.

On the completion of his training he joined the staff of St Christopher's in Temple Road, Cowley, under the headship of Miss Neve.

In 1940 he joined the forces and after his training he had hoped to be a pilot or a navigator, but poor hearing prevented this. After his marriage in 1941 he was posted to Palestine.

After the war Ken returned to St Christopher's. Miss Neve retired and Miss Childs took over as head, with Ken becoming deputy head. He taught the top class in the school and St Christopher's successes in the 11+ examinations were the envy of many of the City's schools.

Ken was keen on sport and was captain of Cowley Cricket Club in 1933 when they won the Telegraph Cup. In the 1934–35 season the school won the junior schools football trophy.

After the war St Christopher's, under Ken's guidance, was a dominant force in the inter-schools competitions at swimming and athletics, winning the boys' and girls' trophies many times.

On the football front he was secretary of the Oxford Schools F.A. for 24 years and was also secretary and treasurer of the Oxford Boys' team, with whom he travelled extensively for many years.

When Miss Childs retired in 1966 it was thought that Ken would become head, but this was not to be and, in 1968, he left St Christopher's to become head at Wood Farm School.

Dennis 'Joe' Banton

Dennis 'Joe' Banton was born in Nottingham in 1930. 'Joe', who had two older brothers, lost his father when he was one year old and, in 1934, the family moved to Phipps Road, Cowley, before finally settling at 49 Temple Road. 'Joe' attended St Christopher's Infants and Junior Schools before passing the 11 plus to gain a place at Southfield School (later Oxford Boys). 'Joe' became a good sportsman from an early age, starting with football and cricket under the guidance of Mr Halsey at St Christopher's school. Rugby took over from football at Southfield and he represented the school at Rugby, Cricket (also captain of the County Colts), Basketball, Athletics and even Chess. On leaving school, 'Joe' gained a place at Borough Road College (later Brunel University), where he was able to continue his sporting pursuits. National service followed college and once again his sporting ability stood him in good stead.

'Joe's' first teaching post on leaving the army came at East Oxford School in 1951. Spells at Margaret Road, Bayswater and St James's Cowley followed before he became deputy head at Summertown School for five years. At the age of 32 'Joe' took the Headship at South Oxford, a position he held until, in 1967, his teaching career finally took him to Temple Cowley, almost back to his roots, where he remained Headmaster for 23 years until his retirement.

'Joe's' teaching success was equalled in the Oxford sporting circles with cricket taking pride of place. As well as a lengthy spell as captain of Cowley St John Cricket Club, 'Joe' also represented the County side, making 208 Minor County appearances, including six seasons as captain, Basketball, Table Tennis and latterly golf and bowls, completing his sporting life. After playing golf at Southfield for a number of years, 'Joe' joined Frilford Heath golf club where he also had a season as captain. At Frilford he was asked why he took up golf and he replied, 'To fill in between cricket and death.'

Gwyn Morgan, Bookmaker

Gwyn Morgan walked to Oxford from South Wales as a young man in 1926, and found work at the Pressed Steel factory. While at the factory he started taking bets and, as the business grew, the front room of the family home in Cranmer Road became a 'bookies'. Many a wife would knock the door to tell Gwynn that their husband had gambled away their wages and there was no money for the children's meals — so she gave it back to them! In 1955 he bought a shop in Between Towns Road and had Licence No. 1 in Oxford.

Gwyn had a passion for boxing and often fought as a lightweight at Oxford Town Hall, as well as being a benefactor to the sport in later years. He is seen here on the left-hand side.

A party of Cowley Old Age Pensioners on a coach outing, paid for courtesy of Gwyn Morgan. His success as a 'bookie' enabled him to own racehorses and greyhounds, but he was always a generous man. He gave the old age pensioners of Cowley a coach outing each year and held Christmas parties for as many as one hundred at a time, who all received a Christmas gift.

John Bunyan Baptist Church, Crowell Road

Worship began on 22 April 1939 in the small hall and was led by the church's first minister, Rev. David Rigden Green. Numbers grew rapidly and the small hall, seating 50-60 worshippers, was inadequate and, with a promise of £1,000 from Lord Nuffield for the erection of a Sunday School, it was agreed to start the building of the main hall on 5 April 1940.

The foundation stone was laid on 1 June 1940, and was opened for worship a year later on 28 June 1941.

The interior of the Baptist Hall in the 1950s. In 1949 a Baptistry had been built by voluntary labour and was situated under the platform. The organ was installed in 1952, having been purchased from All Saints Church, Highfield in Headington. The hall was used for many church activities but it was hoped that a building exclusively for worship would eventually become a reality.

The Rev. Sydney Crowe took up the ministry at John Bunyan in 1942 when the Rev. David Rigden Green left to become an RAF Chaplain. Mr Crowe and his wife, Ivy, remained at Cowley for nearly 30 years and served the community until Sydney Crowe's retirement in 1972. He became Oxford's first minister of religion to serve as a magistrate in 1967. He also served on the Oxford City Education Committee and was a school governor at several local schools. He was twice president of the Oxford Free Church Federal Council.

The Rev. Sydney Crowe and his wife, Ivy, on retirement in 1972, outside the church.

The new church building exclusively for worship was started as the Church celebrated its 25th year, i.e. 1964. The foundation stone was laid in March. Left to right: Rev. Sydney Crowe (minister), Rev. R Childs Principal of Regents Park College, Rev. E Sharpe New Road Church, Rev. D Hicks Area Superintendent.

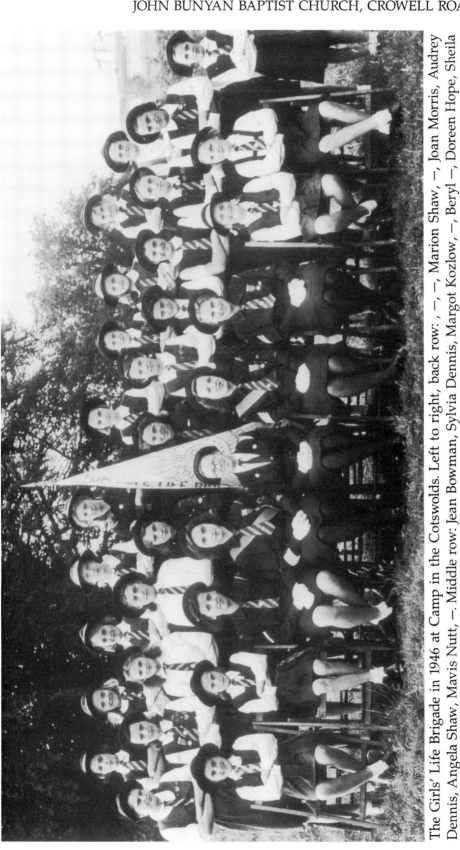

The Girls' Life Brigade in 1946 at Camp in the Cotswolds. Left to right, back row: –, –, Marion Shaw, –, Joan Morris, Audrey Dennis, Angela Shaw, Mavis Nutt, –. Middle row: Jean Bowman, Sylvia Dennis, Margot Kozlow, –, Beryl –, Doreen Hope, Sheila Atkinson, –, Peris Roberts, Kathleen Maskins, Beryl Nellor. Front row: Pat –, Phyllis Rimes, – Simms, Pamela Wallis, Ivy Crowe, Christine Greenaway, Christine Farmer, Pat Jordan, Sheila Eden, Carol Brooks.

The Girls's Life Brigade was the first uniformed group to be established at John Bunyan Church. In 1943 Miss Nellie Alden and Mrs Crowe (captain) held meetings on Saturday afternoons to avoid the black-out and air raids.

The 3rd Oxford Company of the Boys' Brigade

Since 1940 there had been attempts to start an organisation for boys. An early attempt to start a Life Boy Team had been unsuccessful, but when Rev. Crowe took up the ministry in 1942, a Boys' Brigade Company was formed under the leadership of Mr W J Bettam. Mr Bettam held the captaincy until 1948, when Mr J A Hope took over. Both uniformed groups ceased to exist by the 1960s.

The Brigade marching past the John Bunyan church in Crowell Road in 1947.

The first group photograph, dated 1943, showing off the allotments outside the church. Left to right, back row adults: −, Walter Bettam, −, Rev. Crowe, −, Moel Roberts. Boys: −, Peter Crane, −, Chris? Porter, −, Keith Porter, −, −, −, −, −, Eddie Rimes, Aubrey Nellor, −, −, −, −.

The Boys' Brigade Camp 1947. The Cowley group with boys from Cumnor at Herne Bay. Left to right, back row: Chris Porter, –, –, –, –, Gordon Cullimore, Ernie Paintin, Eddie Rimes, George Cook, five unknown. Third row: six unknown, Bob Collins, Keith Porter. Second row: six unknown, Mr Bettam, Mrs Bettam?, –, –, Mr Hope.

The 3rd Oxford Company of Boys' Brigade c1952. Left to right, back row: Harold Welsh, David Joseph, Ian Clamp, Trevor Tate, Jimmy Howells, Joe Hope (captain). Front row: John Skinner, –, –, –, – Jordan, Gilbert Payne. In front: –.

The Young People's Fellowship

Work with young people was a priority in the early days of the Church and the Christian Endeavour was formed in 1940. It remained small and soon joined with the Young People's Fellowship and numbers reached 30 to 40 by the 1960s. The activities were mainly recreational with an annual camp at Hill End. However, they also raised funds for the new church, distributed parcels at Christmas, and chopped wood for the elderly during the winter months.

Young People's Fellowship 1950. Left to right, back row: Mrs Haysom, Marcia Frampton, Mavis Nutt, –, – Brooks, Mrs MacMillan, Marjorie Wagstaff. Middle row: Alan Feast, Gilbert Payne, Beryl Eales, Janet Russin, –, Avril Roberts, –, Jean Clark, Angela Shaw. Front row: Ann Batts, Pat –, –, –.

Young People's Fellowship c1955. Left to right, back row: Michael Cusden, Sam –, Jenny Edwards, David Rogers, Sylvia Taylor, –, Christopher Francis?, –, Hedley Feast, Leslie Barnes. Third row: Elizabeth Hardstaff, Joan Busby, Maureen Edwards, Rosemary Dowle, Rev. Sydney Crowe, Avril Roberts, Mary Welsher, Terry Herbert. Second row: Trevor Tate, David Herbert, Alan Feast, Peris Roberts, Gilbert Payne, Lorna Pinfold, June Taylor, David Crowe. Front row: Josephine Deer, Linda Haynes, Wayne Thomas, Pamela Spindler, Marian McCready, Jean McLaren.

The Summer Fete 1951. This was held on the field next to St James School Hut at the top of Church Street (now Beauchamp Lane). There was a May Queen procession and maypole dancing. Left to right: Avril Roberts, –, –, Joan Busby, –, Peris Roberts (May Queen), –, Gillian McKay, Caroline Chapline, Jean Clark (Herald).

A Sunday School Parade in November 1961. It was decided to advertise the Sunday School to the children of the newly established Airfield Estate. The children are being organised to proceed through the streets.

John Bunyan Church 50th Anniversary, April 1989. Left to right: Jean Clark, John Clark, Mrs Frampton, Mrs Wagstaff, Mrs Welsher, Eva Crane, Mrs Stannard, Mrs Childs? (behind), Reg Crane, Howard Argent, Christine Greenaway, Mr Hope (behind), Mr Stannard, Mrs Davis. In front: Gilbert Payne.

The Women's Fellowship

The work of the women of the Church has been invaluable over the years. It emphasised practical service both within and without the church; the church has been cleaned regularly and gifts of furniture and equipment donated. A willing band of helpers work happily behind the scenes at all events.

Helpers at the Church Fete in 1951. Left to right, back row: Mrs Roberts, Polly Walters, Mrs Williams, Dot Clark, Mrs Frampton, Mrs Edens. Front row: Miss Patterson, –, Vera Roberts, –, Winnie Howells, Helen Davies, Gwen Clark, Olwen Haysom.

In 1964 the 'catering force' provided excellent refreshments at the opening of the new Church. A few of the men have been enlisted to help. Left to right back row: Cecil Bryant, Moel Roberts, Arthur Hobbs, Peris Roberts, Marion Davies, Jean Herbert, Gladys Herbert, Dot Bryant, Mrs Payne, Mrs Nell Busby, Helen Davies, Mrs Rimes, Vera Roberts. Front row: Mrs Cook, Gwen Clark, –, Olive Hope, Mrs Whittle?, Mrs Frampton, Polly Wallis, Ivy Crowe, Winnie Howells, Daisy Reed. Kneeling: Gilbert Payne.

Salesian College, incorporating Our Lady Help of Christians

Salesian College

An aerial view of the Salesian College, a 19th century building first occupied by St Kenelms School, an Anglican Boarding School founded in 1820. In 1906 the premises were taken over by the Franciscan Friars who moved to a site on Iffley Road in 1921, from which time the Salesian Order educated and boarded boys. The school chapel, originally St Kenelms chapel, served the community as a Roman Catholic parish church until the 1960s when Our Lady Help of Christians was build in Holloway. Crescent Road is running left to right, with Junction Road on the right hand side. The property on the extreme left was occupied at one time by Mr Willis and his sister, and was demolished to make way for Crescent Close. Kings Dairy can be seen on the right-hand side of the middle terrace of houses, entered through an alley to the side. The statue in the middle of the quad was that of St Dominic Savio, an Italian, an original pupil of St John Bosco, who founded the Salesian Order in Italy in the mid-1860s. The school's long jump can be seen on the playing field near the bottom, and the small white roofed building in Junction Road was the shelter for the full-time air raid warden, 'Lofty' Windscheffel. The building on the extreme right-hand side was home to the Catholic Young Men's Society.

A modern aerial view of Cowley c1993. The former Salesian College can be seen on the left-hand side, towards the top of the photograph. Oxford Road is on the right-hand side with Elmthorpe Convent at the top. Temple Cowley School and playing fields are at the bottom of the photograph.

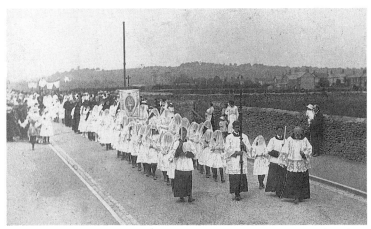

The Blessed Sacrament procession along Junction Road, pre-1914. Cowley Barracks can just be seen in the middle distance.

The Franciscans in the college grounds c1914, during a Corpus Christi procession.

A Corpus Christi procession down Hollow Way, near the junction with Fernhill Road. *'The junction of Hollow Way with Horspath Road used to be known as 'Old Maids Corner' — don't know why, but a lot of old ladies lived there.'*

Our Lady Help of Christians

Our Lady Help of Christians. A May procession in honour of Our Lady in the late 1940s, in Salegate Lane. Back row, left to right: Miss Dagley, Mrs Jones, –, Mrs Ellis, Teresa Pope. Front row: Mrs Roach, Mrs Spicer, Mrs Benwell, Mrs Wright, Mrs Walsh, Mrs Roberts, Mrs Brooks, –, Mrs Honey, Mrs Kilkenny?

Father Thomas McKenna spent almost 40 years building up the parish of Our Lady Help of Christians, in Cowley. He died, aged 81, on 8 February 1986. He left Oxford in the summer of 1980 to return to the Salesian Order community house in Battersea, London, where he first said mass in 1933. Fr. Bernard Higgins, Community Rector 1986 said, 'He will be missed by all of us. He was a very pleasant person, who did a lot of hard work in a quiet sort of way.' When Fr McKenna came to Oxford in 1942 he had just £500 to set up a church, school, hall and club. After 38 years in the parish he had achieved all of that. Between 1980 and 1986 he lived in semi-retirement in Battersea as one of three priests at the Sacred Heart Church.

Sport

Pat Quartermain

Pat Quartermain when captain of Pressed Steel Minors.

Pat moved to Cowley from Garsington when he was seven years old. He attended St Christopher's, St James's and Temple Cowley Schools, and Oxford Secondary Technical School (later Cheney School). He played football for all his school sides and showed promise from an early age.

On leaving school he became an apprentice toolmaker at Pressed Steel Company and played football for the Pressed Steel Minors. Being ambitious, Pat asked Headington United for a trial and joined them as an amateur before turning professional in 1956.

After making 32 first team appearances in the 1955/6 season he was not a regular first team choice. The 1961/2 season saw his emergence as first choice left back and he remained a first team regular until late into the 1966/7 season. He missed the last ten matches of the season through injury and was given a free transfer after only one game in the reserves on his return.

He saw further service with Cambridge United, Nuneaton Borough and Banbury Town.

Appearances for Headington:

1955–62 (Southern League and Cup)	99
1962–69 (Football League and Cup)	206

Cliff Holton

Cliff Holton taking the field for Watford.

Cliff Holton was born in Headington Quarry in 1930. The family moved to Florence Park when Cliff was four years old. He attended St Mary and St John School, Cowley St John, and the Technical School in St Ebbes. Cliff played for his school teams, Oxford Boys and the Oxfordshire Youth Team.

On leaving school he became an apprentice toolmaker at Morris Motors Radiators off the Woodstock Road. After two years he was considering a career in the RAF; however, the war years meant a shortage of older players at Oxford City Football Club, so, at the age of 15, he was able to play in a fairly high class of amateur football.

It was while playing for Oxford City that he was spotted by Arsenal F.C. When offered a place at Arsenal he did not hesitate at a chance of becoming a professional footballer: he never did finish his apprenticeship or join the RAF. He was 17 when he joined Arsenal on 22 October 1947. Two years National Service followed, before returning to Arsenal. He made 210 league and cup appearances for Arsenal, scoring 88 goals. In his time with Arsenal he gained a Division 1 championship medal in 1952/3 and an F.A. Cup Runners Up Medal in 1952. In 1958 Cliff was transferred to Watford for £10,000.

While at Arsenal, Cliff had gone into the engineering business and, two years after joining Watford, his football was on a part-time basis. At Watford he made 166 league and cup appearances, scoring 105 goals.

After Watford he left for Northampton in 1961 and hit a hat-trick on his debut and helped to steer them from the third to second division and then on to Crystal Palace. He saw a brief return to Watford before moving to Charlton Athletic in 1966 in a part exchange deal and £4,000 for Stuart Scullion. From there it was on to Leyton Orient. Injuries became more frequent towards the end of his career and he finally retired from football at the age of 38.

Cliff was an all-round sportsman in his time. He played cricket for Oxfordshire, Essex and Middlesex 2nd XIs. He was also adept at athletics, swimming and diving.

Cowley United Football Club

Cowley United Football Club 1949–50. Left to right, back row: George Cook senior (manager), Ron Dawson, – Jeffries, Tony Lee, Jack Goodenough, Tom Hilsdon (at back), Charlie Kerry, Alf Badger. Middle row: 'Chummy' Gooch, Alan Rogers, Ron Brough, Bert Sherman, Roy Quartermain. Front row: 'Whisky' Porter, George Cook junior, – Hilsdon.

Cowley Boys Club

Cowley Boys Club Under 16s, c1959. Left to right, back row: Pete Kenny, Pete Jacobson, Derek Fisher, John Gardiner, Doug Johnson, Stan Hahn, Phil Collins (manager). Front row: Graham Bentham, Mick Taylor, Trevor Williams, Tony Dalton, Alan Lacey.

Cowley Cricket Club

Winners of the Telegraph Cup, 1933. Left to right, back row: B Scatton, A Collier, C Bevercombe (Hon. Sec.), F Barrett, P Barrett. Middle row: H Bradbury, B Alder, Ken Halsey, D Burrell, J Johnson. Front row: H Surman, R Gurden.

Brasenose and Westfield Sports and Social Club

Football team 1947/48 season. Left to right, back row: Arthur Jones, Graham Walker, Buckett, Mick Soames, Don Cooper, John Warland, Charlie Reeves. Middle row: Don White, Bob Whitford, Brian Lee. Front row: John Padbury, Ben Johnson, 'Meg' Merrilies, Trevor Lewis, B Turley, Raymond Whitford mascot.

Shortly after the Second World War the residents of the Brasenose and Westfield Estate (the Horspath Road/Cranmer Road area) formed a sports and social club. Residents paid into a savings fund, which they used to finance social activities. Outings to the seaside were a great favourite and as many as eight coaches would line up in Cranmer Road for a trip to Bournemouth.

Although the club did not have any headquarters they were able to use facilities at Cowley Barracks for sporting activities.

A Youth Section was formed, where athletics, netball, tennis and football were enjoyed. The club ran until the late 1940s when it ceased to operate.

Brasenose and Westfield Football Club

Brasenose and Westfield League and Cup Winning side of 1957—58. Left to right, back row: 'Joe' Clarke, Ken Peaper, Bob Huckin, John Mackie, Don White, Mick Casey, Bernard Hales. Front row: John Whitford, John Hales, Bob Whitford, Bert Jacobs, Paul Kilbee.

A group of young men in the Horspath Road area of Cowley, some of whom were members of the Youth Club a decade earlier, formed the team in the 1956—57 season to play friendly matches on Sunday mornings.

Following a successful season it was decided to try for league football. On behalf of the players, Don White, who was to become secretary and treasurer, and a driving force behind the team, approached the league committee. After passing the vetting procedure the club entered division two of the Oxford City Junior League for the 1957—58 season.

Brasenose and Westfield took the league title and in the League Division II Cup Final trounced Oxford Co-op Sports 8 goals to nil. The club was promoted straight to the Premier Division where they remained until the club folded in the early 1960s.

An *Oxford Mail* cartoon by Alan Course celebrating the 8 goals to nil cup win over Oxford Co-op Sports.

Florence Park

The main gates of Florence Park 1936.

The Estate was built in 1933, primarily for the immigrants who came to work at the car factories. There were so many Welshmen that the estate became known as 'Little Rhondda'. The houses were built by N Moss & Son Limited and on 7 May 1934 the land for Florence Park was given by F E Moss to the Mayor, Aldermen and Citizens of Oxford for use as a public pleasure park. It was named Florence Park after Mr Moss's sister, Florence, and was opened on 28 July 1936.

Betty Radburn, née Durrant, with daughter Elizabeth in 1950. The Coronation Avenue of trees can be seen in the background.

Donnington School opened in 1936 for 388 juniors and 292 infants. The May Queen in 1937 was Betty Durrant.

VE Day Street Party, 1945, outside Nos. 3, 5, 7 and 9 Cornwallis Road, Florence Park Estate.

Florence Park Community Centre Wives Club outing to Jobs Dairy at Didcot, in 1958. Left to right, back row: Jean Philpotts, –, –, –, Mrs Sinnett. Middle row: Sally Harris, Milly Brooks, Cynthia Hutchinson, Elsie Smith. Front row: Mrs McCormack, Mrs Thompson, Audrey Hutchinson, Margaret Fryer with Philip, Jean Warne, –, Jean Cox with Philip, Van Tyler with Susan.

Florence Park Playgroup Nativity Play, at the Community Centre in 1975. Left to right: Thomas McDonagh and Ian Griffiths (Kings), Tina Phipps (Mary), Andrew Clarkson (Joseph).

Coronation Street Party, 1953. Left to right, back row: Jean Philpott, Mrs Holden, Lucy Poulter, Audrey Hutchinson. Middle row: Linda Philpott, Linda Poulter, Maureen Holden, Wendy Hutchinson. In front: Peter Barson, John Thewell.

The Community Centre Revue was an annual event which continued from 1977, when it started in celebration of the Silver Jubilee of Queen Elizabeth. This concert of 1980 shows Dennis Moore and Alan Laitte.

Floods in Campbell Road in 1989.

Fred White, known as 'Fred the Milk', the Florence Park milkman for over 40 years, pictured 6th September 1990, on his retirement from Co-Op Dairy, with, left to right: Sheila Tree, Fred White, Van Tyler, Gladys Curtis.

Material for this section on Florence Park has been kindly donated by Mrs Sheila Tree. The development of the Florence Park Estate is being fully documented and will form a book within the Changing Faces series. Further material, particularly photographs, is needed for inclusion in this book, to be published Christmas 2000.

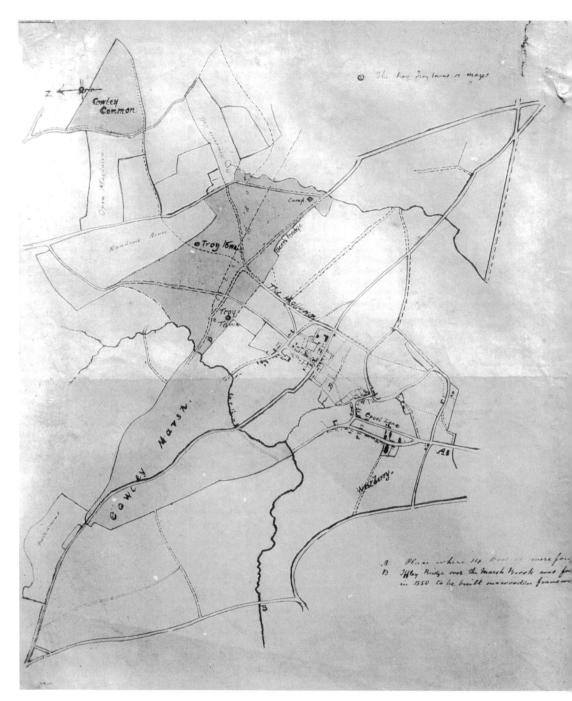

Cowley before the enclosure of 1850. Handwritten comments on this map indicate a point marked 'A' on the map, to the right of Cruel Lane, where *'14 bodies were found'*. Point 'B' comments *'Iffley Bridge over the Marsh Brook was formed in 1850 to be built over wooden framework'*.

A plan of Cowley in the 1960s

The tremendous growth of Cowley from the 1920s to the 1960s can be seen here. Every available space was used for housing development to accommodate the vast number of immigrants, who came to work in the factories. During the late 1950s and 60s, the village was redeveloped and the old village of Middle Cowley or Hockmore Street virtually disappeared.

1. Florence Park Estate
2. Rosehill Estate
3. Sunnyside Estate

4. Airfield Estate
5. Westbury Estate
6. Cowley Centre

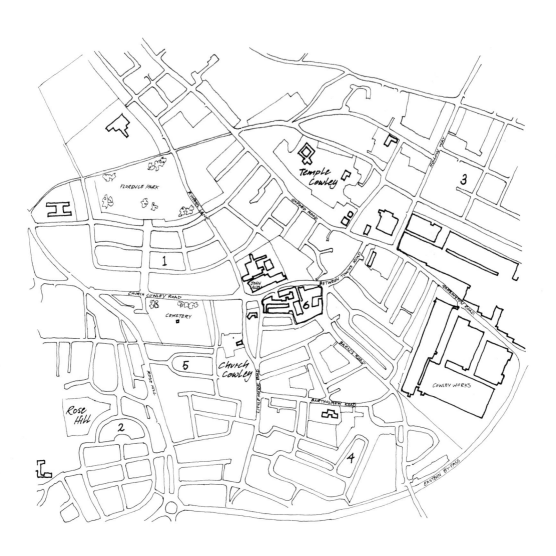

Celebrations

The organising committee of the Cowley Feast 1957. Left to right, back row: Mr F Beardmore, Mr J Phillips (chairman of the Social and Entertainments Committee), Mr R J Spong, Mr W P Welch (warden, Cowley Community centre and organising secretary), Mr F Clayton, Mr C Beasley, Mr T Sainsbury, Mr C W Joel. Front row: Mrs Clayton, Mrs Phillips, Mrs Spong, Mrs D M Cook, Mrs Beasley. In 1957 the Feast attracted 8,400 visitors, compared with just under 7,000 in 1956.

The Cowley Feast was a major social event at Cowley. It was a celebration of the dedication of the Parish Church of St James, and was held on the first Sunday in October in a large field opposite Gibbons Bakery in the High Street (now Between Towns Road), and sometimes in a field off the New Road (now Church Cowley Road), where Florence Park Estate now stands.

A Cowley Feast activity on Saturday 10 October 1955, with P Franklin climbing the 'greasy pole'. The prize for the highest climber was a joint of meat.

A great many people attended the Cowley Feast and the Grand Draw of 1958 advertised a 1st Prize of £5 worth of Premium Bonds.

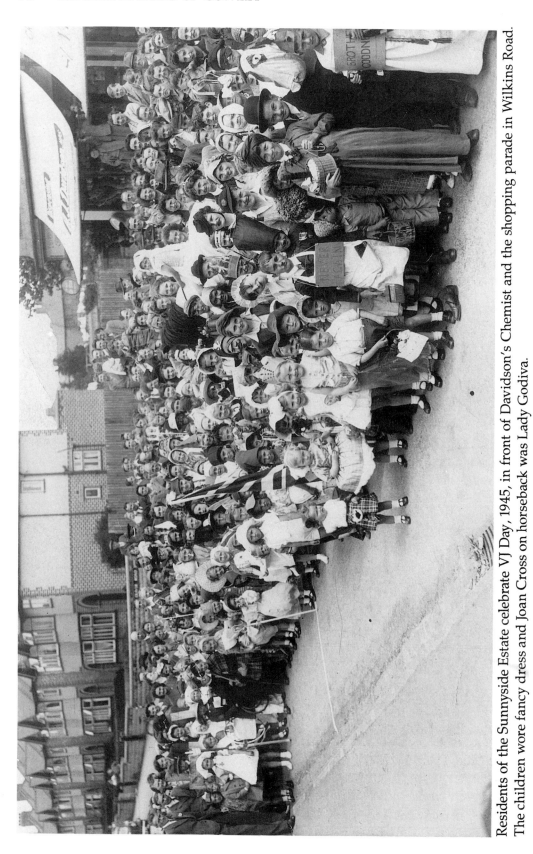

Residents of the Sunnyside Estate celebrate VJ Day, 1945, in front of Davidson's Chemist and the shopping parade in Wilkins Road. The children wore fancy dress and Joan Cross on horseback was Lady Godiva.

Four young local teenagers with birthdays in close proximity celebrate with a combined party held at the Forum Ballroom in Oxford, c1948. Left to right, front row: June Cross (Newman Road), John White (Fern Hill Road), Joan Cross (Wilkins Road), and Brenda Gannon (Fern Hill Road).

Daphne Miles Dancing Class c1950. This class was held every Saturday morning in the Congregational Church on Oxford Road. Left to right, back row: −, −, −, Maureen Edwards, −, −, −Beesley, Susanne Slack, −, Sylvia Taylor, −, −. Third row: Heather Tappin, −, Beryl Yeatman, −, −, Caroline Smith, −, −, Patricia Taylor. Second row: Linda Hickman, −, Christine Howarth, −, Pamela Bennett. Front row: unknown.

Coronation Carnival at Cowley, 1953.